Comprehension

Introductory Book

John Jackman

FOCUS on Comprehension

Using this book

This book will help you to develop your reading skills so that you understand and enjoy what you read even more. You will not only learn to read the lines, but to read between the lines and beyond them as well!

What's in a unit

Each unit is set out in the same way as the example here.

Unit heading ——
This tells you about the text you will be reading

Do you remember ——
Activities to practise and check your understanding

More to think about ——
Activities to practise and develop your understanding

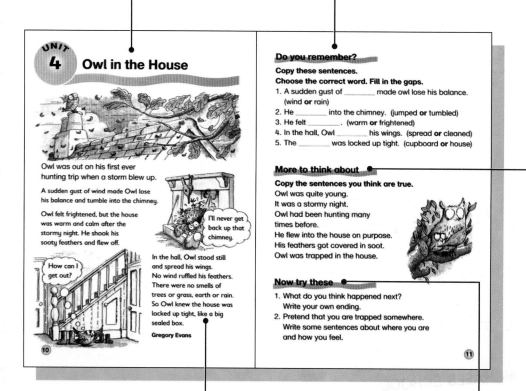

The text ——
The texts have been carefully selected to demonstrate all major genre types, from fiction to non-fiction

Now try these ——
Activities to stretch and extend your understanding

Contents

Unit		Page
1	Hiding	4
2	The Picnic	6
3	Our Dog	8
4	Owl in the House	10
5	Looking After Your Bike	12
6	Gingerbread Man	14
7	Hippo and Monkey	16
8	When I Was One	18
9	Looking at a Dictionary	20
10	Judy and the Martian	22
11	Monkey Business	24
12	When the Wind Blows	26
13	A Very Busy Day	28
Progress Test	Two Legs or Four?	30

Hiding

Under a bush in the garden
is a very good place to hide.

So is a big umbrella,
or down at the end of a bed.

Sometimes Dad hides behind a newspaper.
And Mum hides behind a book on the sofa.

You can even hide under a hat.

Tortoises hide inside their shells
when they aren't feeling friendly,
and hamsters hide right at the
back of their cages when they
want to go to sleep.

When the baby hides his eyes he thinks you can't see him.
But he's there all the time.

Shirley Hughes

Do you remember?

Copy these sentences.
Fill in the right word from the story.

1. Where is the boy hiding?
   The boy is hiding under the _____ .

2. Where is the girl hiding?

The girl is hiding under the _____ .

3. Which animals are hiding in their shells?

_____ are hiding in their shells.

4. Who is hiding behind a newspaper?

_____ is hiding behind a newspaper.

More to think about

Read these sentences about the story.
Copy the sentences that are true.

Under a bush is a bad place to hide.

Dad is hiding behind his newspaper.

Mum is sitting on the floor.

Tortoises hide in their shells.

The baby thinks you can't see him.

Now try these

Write a sentence to answer each question.

1. Why do you think Dad hides behind his newspaper?

2. Why does the baby think you can't see him
   when he hides his eyes?

3. Where is your favourite hiding place?

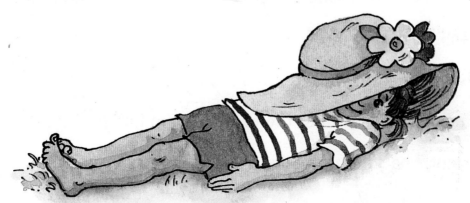

UNIT 2 The Picnic

"Here's a good spot," said Uncle Ben.

Tim and I helped Gran out of the car.

"Oh dear!" said Gran. "My poor old legs get stiff in that car."

It was a very good spot for a picnic. There was lots of dry grass, and there were trees to climb. We could hear the sound of a stream through the bushes.

"Don't you two run off yet," called Mum.
"I need your help to unload the car. You can get the chairs out."

"But, Mum!" said Tim.

"No 'buts', just get on with it," said Mum.

"Yes, come on, Tim, let's get the food out. I'm hungry," I said.

"Oh, all right," he said grumpily.

Do you remember?

| Ben   chairs   five   Gran   trees |

Choose a word from the box to answer each question.
1. What was the uncle's name?
2. Who was the oldest person at the picnic?
3. How many people were there?
4. What might the children climb?
5. What did Mum ask the children to get from the car?

More to think about

Write a sentence to answer each question.

1. What did Gran grumble about?
2. Why did the children think it was a good place for a picnic?
3. How do we know it hadn't been raining?
4. Why couldn't they see the stream from the picnic spot?
5. Why do you think Tim said, "But, Mum"?

Now try these

1. Make a list of the things that you need to take on a picnic.
2. Write about what you think the children did after they had eaten their picnic.

UNIT 3 Our Dog

Our dog has to go for walks every day.
She stares at us until we take her.

One day she found a smelly pond
and jumped into it.
"Pooh! You smell disgusting!"
we told her.

Then she rolled in the mud.
"Pretend she's not ours," whispered Mum.
"We must get her home quickly and give her a bath."

We made her wait outside the kitchen door.
Mum filled the bath.
"I'll put her in," Mum said.
"Now hold on tight!
"Don't let her jump out!"

Helen Oxenbury

Do you remember?

bath	mud	day	smelly

Copy these sentences.
Choose a word from the box to fill each gap.
1. The dog has a walk every _____ .
2. One day she jumped in a _____ pond.

8

3. She also rolled in the _____ .

4. They took the dog home and gave her a _____ .

More to think about

Read these sentences about the story.
Write 'true' or 'not true' for each one.

1. The dog has a walk once a week.

2. She barks when she wants a walk.

3. The dog likes water.

4. Sometimes she gets herself muddy.

5. She has a bath in the kitchen.

6. The dog sits quietly in the bath.

Now try these

**The instructions for bathing the dog are in the wrong order.
Write them in the right order.**

Dry her with a towel.

Rinse off all the soap.

Splash the water onto the dog's coat.

Fill the bath with warm water.

Lift the dog into the water.

Rub shampoo into her wet coat.

Draw a picture of the dog in the bath.
Make up a name for the dog.
Under the picture write the dog's name.

Owl in the House

Owl was out on his first ever hunting trip when a storm blew up.

A sudden gust of wind made Owl lose his balance and tumble into the chimney.

Owl felt frightened, but the house was warm and calm after the stormy night. He shook his sooty feathers and flew off.

I'll never get back up that chimney.

How can I get out?

In the hall, Owl stood still and spread his wings. No wind ruffled his feathers. There were no smells of trees or grass, earth or rain. So Owl knew the house was locked up tight, like a big sealed box.

Gregory Evans

Do you remember?

Copy these sentences.
Choose the correct word. Fill in the gaps.

1. A sudden gust of _____ made owl lose his balance. (wind **or** rain)
2. He _____ into the chimney. (jumped **or** tumbled)
3. He felt _____. (warm **or** frightened)
4. In the hall, Owl _____ his wings. (spread **or** cleaned)
5. The _____ was locked up tight. (cupboard **or** house)

More to think about

Copy the sentences you think are true.
Owl was quite young.
It was a stormy night.
Owl had been hunting many
times before.
He flew into the house on purpose.
His feathers got covered in soot.
Owl was trapped in the house.

Now try these

1. What do you think happened next?
   Write your own ending.
2. Pretend that you are trapped somewhere.
   Write some sentences about where you are
   and how you feel.

Looking After Your Bike

A bike is a machine.
All machines need to be looked after carefully.

Tips for looking after your bike

- Clean and dry your bike when it is
wet or muddy.
Then it won't get rusty.
Use polish to make it really shine!

- Ask someone to help you to check the brakes.
The brakes are very important for your safety.

- Be sure that there is enough air in the tyres.

- Make sure the seat is at the correct height
for you.
You should be able to touch the ground
with both feet.

- Oil the chain, pedals and levers.
Don't get oil on the wheels where the
brakes touch, or the brakes won't work.

- Always wear your helmet when you
ride your bike.
Remember to keep your helmet clean.

Be proud of your bike,
and be proud of the way you ride it!

Do you remember?

Copy the sentences you think are true.

A bike is a machine.

All bikes are red.

Bikes get rusty if they are left out in the rain.

Tyres do not need air in them.

You need to keep your bike well oiled.

Every bike rider should wear a helmet.

More to think about

Write a sentence to answer each question.

1. Why do you need to keep your bike dry?
2. Why are brakes very important?
3. How can you tell if your seat is the correct height?
4. Which parts of your bike need to be oiled?
5. What should you always wear when riding your bike?

Now try these

1. Pretend it is your birthday. You have been given a new bike. Describe what it is like.
2. Make a list of the good things about having a bike.
3. Write the main safety rules for bike riders. One is done to help you.

1 Always wear a helmet.
2
3
4
5
6

UNIT 6 Gingerbread Man

One day Gran made a gingerbread man for the children. But as she opened her oven, up jumped the gingerbread man and off he ran.

"Stop, stop," called the cat.
"Let's have a chat."

"Oh no, not me.
"No one's eating me for tea,"
he shouted, and on he ran.
On and on ran the little man.

"Stop, stop," called the bird.
"Let's have a word."

"Oh no, not me.
"No one's eating me for tea," he shouted, and on he ran.
On and on ran the little man.

But then the gingerbread man came to a big, wide lake.

"I can help," said the old fox.
"I will carry you across the lake."
"Sit on my tail," said the old fox.
"Sit on my back," said the old fox.
"Sit on my nose," said the old fox.

Traditional tale

Do you remember?

Copy these sentences.
Choose the correct word. Fill in each gap.

1. The gingerbread man jumped from the _____.
   (oven **or** cupboard)
2. First he ran past the _____. (cat **or** rat)
3. On he ran past the _____. (chicken **or** bird)
4. When he reached the _____ he stopped. (hill **or** lake)
5. A _____ said he would help. (fish **or** fox)

More to think about

Look at these sentences. Copy them in the right order.
The first one has been done to help you.

The bird tried to stop the gingerbread man.
He ran past the cat.
He came to the lake.
The gingerbread man jumped from the oven.
Gran made a gingerbread man.

1 Gran made a gingerbread man.

Now try these

1. Pretend you are the gingerbread man.
   Write about how you feel when you come to the lake.
2. Write the reasons why you think the gingerbread man
   can't cross the lake by himself.
3. Write your own ending for the story.
   Try to make it a surprise.

UNIT 7

Hippo and Monkey

Hippo was the strongest of all the animals, so he said he should be Chief. The other animals didn't want Hippo as their Chief. He was too grumpy and moody.

"I bet I can get you out of the pool, Hippo," called Monkey.
"I bet you can't," grunted Hippo.
"I'm the strongest animal in the world."
"If I can get you out of the pool, then I should be Chief," said Monkey.
"If you can get me out of the pool, then you can be Chief," said Hippo, "but if I get you into the pool, you will be my servant – for ever!"

Off went Monkey to get a really strong rope.
"Hold tight to the rope," said Monkey, "but don't pull until I shout."

Monkey ran into the trees with the other end of the rope.
All the animals watched.
Monkey tied the rope to a big, strong tree trunk.
"Pull!" shouted Monkey. "Pull!"
"This will be easy," thought Hippo to himself.

But all day and all night Hippo pulled, while Monkey sat and ate bananas, and snoozed! Hippo was getting very tired and cross, very cross indeed.
"That monkey must be the strongest monkey I've ever known," thought Hippo.

Slowly he climbed out of the pool, to try to see Monkey.

Just as Hippo took his last foot out of the pool, Monkey ran out of the trees ...

Nigerian folk tale retold by John Jackman

Do you remember?

Write 'yes' or 'no' for each of these sentences.

1. Monkey thought he was the strongest animal in the world.
2. Monkey played a trick on Hippo.
3. Hippo liked to sit in the pool all day.
4. All the animals helped Monkey to pull the rope.
5. While Hippo pulled, Monkey ate bananas.

More to think about

Sort the words in the box into two lists.
Two have been done to help you.

brown grey huge fat clever moody grumpy small thin

Words that describe Monkey	Words that describe Hippo
brown	grey

Now try these

1. Write the end of the story in your own words.
2. Who was more clever, Hippo or Monkey?
   Say why you think this.

When I Was One

When I was One,
I had just begun.
When I was Two,
I was nearly new.
When I was Three,
I was hardly me.
When I was Four,
I was not much more.
When I was Five,
I was just alive.
But now I am Six,
I'm as clever as clever.
So I think I'll be Six now
for ever and ever.

A.A.Milne

Do you remember?

Copy these sentences.
Choose a word from the picture to fill each gap.
1. There are six candles on the _____ .
2. The _____ is under the table.
3. The boy hasn't opened his _____ yet.
4. Four _____ have come to his party.
5. There are bunches of _____ on the wall.

More to think about

Write the answers to these rhyming questions.
1. Find a word in the poem to rhyme with these words.
   The first one has been done for you.
   a) one … begun   b) two … _____
   c) three … _____   d) four … _____
   e) five … _____
2. Write a different word of your own
   to rhyme with these words.
   a) one   b) two   c) three

Now try these

1. Write a list of the five things
   you like best about birthdays.
2. Write a list of three things you
   don't like about birthdays.

UNIT 9

Looking at a Dictionary

Here is a page from a dictionary.
Dictionaries tell us what words mean.
They also help us to spell words.

ever always, for all time
every all, one
examination 1) a test
   2) a close look
excellent very, very good
excuse a reason for doing
   (or not doing) something
expect to think something
   will happen
explode to blow up
eye the part of the body
   you see with

Ff

face 1) the front part of
   the head
   2) to look towards
fact something that is true
factory a building where
   things are made
fail 1) not to do something
   you try to do
   2) to break down
fair 1) a show or market
   2) blond or light in colour
   3) just, honest
fall to drop down

Do you remember?

Look at the words in thick black print.
Write the answers to these questions in your book.
1. How many words begin with e?
2. How many words begin with f?

3. Which is the first word that begins with e?
4. Which is the last word that begins with f?

More to think about

Answer these questions about the dictionary page.
1. What are the two things we can use a dictionary for?
2. Copy what these words mean:
    a) excellent   b) expect   c) explode
    d) fact   e) factory   f) fall
3. Which words have two different meanings?
4. Which word has three different meanings?

Now try these

1. Copy the lists of words and meanings.
    Draw lines to match them.
    One has been done to help you.

    Word   **Meaning**
    examination   not to do something you try to do
    excuse   the part of the body you see with
    eye ————————————something that is true
    fact ——————   a reason for doing or not doing
    fail   something
                           a test
2. Write a meaning for each of these words.
    Check your answers in a dictionary.
    a) acorn   b) blow   c) canal
    d) dislike   e) enjoy   f) free

Judy and the Martian

It was the middle of the night when the rocket landed in the supermarket car park. The engine had failed. The hatch opened and the Martian peered out. A Martian, I should tell you, has webbed feet, green skin and eyes on the ends of horns like a snail. This one, who was three hundred and twenty-seven years old, wore a red jersey.

He said, "Bother!" He had only passed his driving test the week before and was already losing his way.

He was also an extremely nervous person, and felt the cold badly. He shivered. A car hooted and he scuttled behind a rubbish bin.

It began to rain. He wrapped himself in a newspaper but the rain soon came through that. And then he saw that a sliding door into the back of the supermarket had been left a little bit open, just enough for him to wriggle through.

Penelope Lively

Do you remember?

Copy these sentences. Choose the correct ending. Write each in your book.

1. The rocket landed
   - in a car park.
   - in a field.
   - in a garden.

2. The Martian had
- red skin.
- blue skin.
- green skin.

3. He was
- 273 years old.
- 327 years old.
- 723 years old.

4. When it rained he
- climbed into the rubbish bin.
- got into his rocket.
- went into the supermarket.

More to think about

Write a sentence to answer each of these questions.

1. Why did the rocket land in the car park?
2. What did the Martian look like?
3. When did the Martian pass his driving test?
4. Why did he scuttle behind a rubbish bin?
5. How did the Martian get into the supermarket?

Now try these

1. Draw a picture of the Martian standing next to his rocket in the car park.
   Write some sentences about how he feels in this strange new world.
2. Which word in the story means:
   a) broken down   b) an opening like a small door
   c) very, very   d) ran with little steps
   e) to twist and turn

Monkey Business

Here is a story from a newspaper.

CHEEKY CHIMPS ON THE MOTORWAY

Drivers were surprised to see monkeys running all over the road yesterday. The lorry taking them to their new home at Burwell Zoo had broken down. While the driver went to get help, one of the monkeys managed to lift the latch on the door. Inspector Baker said the monkeys thought it was great fun. They climbed all over the road signs and scrambled up the lampposts. They even sat on top of the police car! Some drivers got cross because of the traffic jam, but most drivers thought it was funny.

"I'm pleased to say all the cheeky chimps are now safely back in the zoo," said Inspector Baker last night.

Do you remember?

Copy these sentences. Choose the correct word.

1. The monkeys escaped from a _____ .
   (ship **or** lorry **or** train)
2. It was taking them to a _____ .
   (forest **or** zoo **or** circus)
3. They got out through the _____ .
   (door **or** window **or** roof)
4. _____ of the car drivers thought
   it was funny. (Most **or** all **or** none)
5. The police inspector called them _____ _____ .
   (cheeky chimps **or** silly sausages **or** mad monkeys)

More to think about

Answer these questions in your book.

1. Where were the chimps being taken?
2. Do you think the chimps were pleased to be
   out of the lorry? Why?
3. How did the monkeys get out of the lorry?
4. Why were some of the drivers cross?

Now try these

1. Think of an animal you would like to be.
   Write some sentences to say why.
2. Pretend that you are a rabbit living in a hutch all day.
   You can see children playing in the garden.
   Write about how you might feel.

When the Wind Blows

When the wind blows
Coats flap, scarves flutter.

When the wind blows
Branches groan, leaves mutter.

When the wind blows
Curtains swish, papers scatter.

When the wind blows
Gates creak, dustbins clatter.

When the wind blows
Doors slam, windows rattle.

When the wind blows
Inside is a haven
Outside is a battle.

John Foster

Do you remember?

Copy these sentences.
Choose a word from the box to fill each gap.

scatter	mutter	flutter	clatter

1. When the wind blows scarves _____.
2. When the wind blows leaves _____.

3. When the wind blows papers _____ .
4. When the wind blows dustbins _____ .

More to think about

Write 'always', 'sometimes', or 'never' for each of these sentences

1. On windy days chimneys get blown off roofs.
2. On windy days it is freezing cold going to school.
3. On windy days the sun shines.
4. On windy days the air doesn't move.
5. On windy days ships get wrecked.
6. On windy days flags flap in the breeze.

Now try these

1. Imagine it is a very windy day. Make two lists in your book, like this:

Things I **like** about windy days	Things I **dislike** about windy days

2. What is your favourite weather?
   Say why you like it best.

A Very Busy Day

When someone asks you, "What did you do today?" tell them you have been very, very busy.

After all...

Your hair grew.

Your teeth cut and chewed food.

Your nose smelled smells.

You took in air.

You took goodness from the food you ate.

Your skin stopped germs getting inside you.

Your skeleton moved hundreds of times.

Your muscles moved your bones.

Your heart pumped blood around your body.

Your brain looked after everything you did.

Yes, you and your body have been very busy today!

Martin Skelton and David Playfoot

Do you remember

Copy the sentences you think are true.

Our hair is growing all the time.

We take in air through our ears.

We must eat food to live.

All the bones in our bodies make
our skeletons.

Our brains are very important.

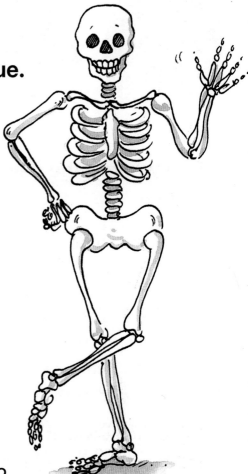

More to think about

**Write the answer to each question
in a sentence.**

1. What do we use our teeth for?
2. What does our nose do?
3. What stops germs getting inside us?
4. How are our bones moved?
5. What pumps the blood around our bodies?

Now try these

1. Draw a picture of yourself. Write these labels on
   the picture.

   | head | knee | ankle | elbow |

   | shoulder | neck | chest |

2. Make a list of five rules to help you keep healthy.
   One is done to help you.
   1. Always wash your hands before eating food.

Two Legs or Four?

Ben wanted the new puppy to have the same name as him.

"It's going to be very confusing," said Dad.

In fact, as time went by, they found it rather useful to have both the son and dog with the same name. Ben spent all day with Ben, and the same words served for both.

"Be quiet, Ben!" for instance, stopped one yelling and the other yapping, and both came when the name was called, and sat down when they were ordered, and each looked equally pleased when told "What a good boy, Ben!"

And indeed Ben was a good boy or rather a good puppy. He never made messes on the carpet, he never chewed curtains or covers, he ate well and he slept soundly as night. As well as learning the ordinary things that dogs learn, he took to copying everything the boy did.

If Ben laughed, Ben barked.

If Ben cried, Ben howled.

If Ben lost his temper and roared angrily, Ben growled.

And one day, would you believe it,
Mum looked out of the window
to see, not one, but two Bens
turning somersaults on
the lawn.

Sometimes, of course, there was
confusion, like:

"I took Ben to have his jabs today."

"To the doctor or the vet?"

Or: "Ben wants a biscuit."

"Custard cream or Bonio?"

Or: "Ben's been ever so good today."

"Good boy or good dog?"

Dick King-Smith

Do you remember?

Write the correct answer to each question in your book.

1. What new pet did the family have?

   a) They had a kitten.   b) They had a puppy.

2. Who wanted the new pet to be called Ben?

   a) Mum wanted it called Ben.

   b) Ben wanted it called Ben.

3. How did the puppy behave?
   a) It was a good puppy.
   b) It was a naughty puppy.
4. Did the puppy mess on the carpets?
   a) Yes, the puppy messed on the carpets.
   b) No, the puppy never messed on the carpets.

More to think about

Write a sentence to answer each question.
1. Why was it useful to have the boy and the puppy with the same name?
2. What did the puppy do when the boy laughed?
3. What did the puppy do when the boy lost his temper?
4. Why do you think the puppy took to copying everything the boy did?
5. Name one of the problems that came from both being called Ben.

Now try these

1. Pretend that you have just been given a new pet. Draw a picture of it.
   Write about how you feel and how you will look after it.
2. Find words in the story that mean:
   a) becoming mixed up
   b) shouting
   c) giving an order
   d) the same amount
   e) crossly
   f) rolling head-over-heels.